Engineering – U

A Guide to the Engineering Student Life

Chad D. Carpenter

Copyright © 2014 Chad D Carpenter

All rights reserved.

ISBN: 1501073842

ISBN-13: 978-1501073847

DEDICATION

To all the family, friends, and educators that challenged me to raise my own standard.

CONTENTS

Introduction to the World of Engineering	*1*
Finding Your Niche	*15*
Have an End-Goal	*29*
Surviving the Engineering Student Life	*44*
Strong Body, Strong Mind	*53*
Internships and Co-op Programs	*60*
Skills Every Engineer Needs But Are Not Taught	*73*
Divide and Conquer	*96*

Introduction to the World of Engineering

"Scientists dream about doing great things. Engineers do them." – James. A Michener

So you have decided, or you are at least considering becoming an engineer. Or maybe someone gave you this book as a subtle hint to think about some upcoming life choices. I'm sure they had good intentions. Either way, I am excited to share with you the evolution of student to engineer. The life of an engineer can offer so many great experiences, challenges, and accomplishments. However, some confusion, hardships, and failures also come along, but do not let that discourage you. Engineering is a profession held with high regards for a reason. If it was easy, everyone would do it. Then nobody would think much of an engineer, and I would probably be writing about how to become a chef (my back-up career plan).

This book is targeted at anyone who is considering going to school to become an engineer or is well on his or her way. Some of the information may apply to the general population of college students, but I will supply additional considerations for those in engineering fields. Do not interpret that you need to be a high-school senior or college freshmen to gain something from this book. While they may be the majority of the audience, if this book can give confidence to an untraditional student that may be a few years out of high school, someone who has already invested a few college semesters into a totally different major, or someone who is a middle-aged wage employee considering a career change, I am more than thrilled. I want to expose you to what engineers actually do and the process it takes to get there. There are also additional chapters supplying some advice on studying effectively, getting your first engineering job, and how to keep your sanity with plenty emphasis on having fun. It is college after all, and you should have fun. Most of the information provided is a collection of general knowledge, technical studies, opinions of current engineers, and the author's first-hand experience. If you find something you don't agree with or if you flat out don't enjoy the book, then I'm sure you could still use this this book to put under that unleveled table or chair you have around the house. That would be the "engineer" thing to do.

The Engineering Stereotype – Fact or Fiction?

For most of the upcoming generation, when you hear engineer, the first thing that comes to mind is the nerdy comic loving, bowl-cut wearing Howard Wolowitz from the TV series *The Big Bang Theory*. Even with his cheesy pick-up lines and obnoxious mother, he still manages to marry a beautiful woman and become an astronaut. That's not a terrible life in my opinion. There is no doubt that engineers like Howard exist and thrive in that personality, but it is a very narrow perception of an engineer. Before *The Big Bang Theory*, society viewed engineers as the pocket protector wearing, socially awkward office workers such as depicted by Scott Adam's *Dilbert*. Although Dilbert has quite a talent for sarcasm, he is still far from the truth of how real engineers behave. This is because engineers are some of the most diverse people.

To help make my case, let's go through some well-known engineers of sorts that are better known for much other accomplishments and personalities. President Hoover was actually a mining engineer before going into politics. President Jimmy Carter also dabbled in nuclear engineering and reactor technology while in the Navy. Is president not bold enough for you? How about the supermodel bombshell Cindy Crawford? She studied chemical engineering before going into modeling. There is also the rocker Tom Sholz of Boston who earned a bachelor's and master's degree in mechanical engineering from the prestigious Massachusetts Institute for Technology (MIT). For the younger generation, some of these names may be before your time. Before taking an acting career, the tech savvy Ashton Kutcher studied biochemical engineering. What about genius billionaire, philanthropist Tony Stark? Yes, I know he is fictional, but who do you think Robert Downey Jr. studied to prepare for the role of Iron Man? That would be Space X CEO Elon Musk. Although he actually has bachelor degrees in economics and physics, he is the epitome of engineer and takes an active design and development role in his companies on top of being a CEO. Hmmm, it seems we are missing some athletes. Oh wait, there have been several Heisman Trophy winners that were engineering students.

Engineering is for all personalities and backgrounds. Just about the only common trait engineers share is their natural curiosity for how systems do work and how systems could work. We are those children that stick objects into power outlets. Sure it's dangerous, but remember the story of Benjamin Franklin holding a kite in the middle of lightning storm? Now that was crazy and dangerous, but also incredibly bold. You should take the nerdy perception with a grain of salt. Yes, we do tend to 'nerd out' when we talk about something that we are passionate about, but so does everyone else of all other professions. First thing to come to mind is a football analyst on TV when his team scores. Engineers still like sports, but we also get excited when talking about engines and computers. Those who tend to nerd out more than others are the lucky ones because they are truly experiencing something they enjoy more than others. If you are happy with being the classic nerd, then that is great. If that image just isn't you, then that shouldn't stop you from becoming an engineer. Engineers can also be charming, funny, athletic, and an adventurist. Just the other day, I found myself white water rafting down the Ocoee River. Six out of the seven passengers were engineers, and five of those were working on a masters or PhD. The single non-engineer, seventh passenger and our river guide – self-educated techie who worked as a sales associate for a robotics company.

What Engineers Actually Do (and what they DON'T do).

One of the hardest questions engineers face on a daily basis is "What do you actually do?" The answer can be so complex and long-winded to the point that the person asking regrets ever bringing it up. More oddly, you could ask that same question to two engineers with the same degree and employer, and you could get two completely different answers. So let's make this simple. An engineer can really be summed up in two words: *problem solver*. Engineers take a problem, apply their technical knowledge and intuition, and then compose a solution. So maybe *technical problem solver* is a more adequate description. Often, the title of 'engineer' and 'scientist' can overlap in their general job descriptions, especially in the areas of research and development. Traditionally, scientist are more geared towards the pure physical sciences and look for explanations of the physical phenomena of chemistry, biology, and physics, but this is not always the case in the modern industry. Engineers can be viewed as scientists that take the current knowledge of physical sciences and look for ways to make a process better or apply a known process in a totally different manner. Take the Archimedes screw for example. It was a rotating spiral wedge that was originally designed to bring water up from a lower to higher elevation. Now this same invention is used for fastening screws, drills, and even propellers! You will find engineers in most of the typical places you would expect such as research labs, power plants, manufacturing plants, etc. However, you can also find engineers working in hospitals, courtrooms, and even cockpits. So let's go through a few disciplines of engineering to get a better description of what engineers do.

The Spectrum of Engineers

Engineering covers a wide range of technical subjects without any clear distinction between the common disciplines offered at universities. The following descriptions are of the common disciplines, but are not the limit to what engineering contains. Some schools offer specialty disciplines such as Mining Engineering, Petroleum Engineering, or Agricultural Engineering while other schools highly encourage students to become interdisciplinary amongst the common disciplines. I will try to name a few discipline specific courses for each discipline so that you gain an idea of classes to expect. Also, the descriptions supplied for each discipline may not entirely satisfy what the engineering discipline fully encompasses, but the description will be a high level overview. Every school goes about the curriculums a little differently, so it's hard to give a 'one-size-fits-all' description. I encourage the reader to browse through all the disciplines, but feel free to skip those that do not seem to interest you.

Aerospace/Mechanical Engineering

Some who are new to engineering may be wondering why I have put aerospace engineering and mechanical engineering in the same description. In reality, mechanical and aerospace curriculums contain many of the same principles. It's quite often that aerospace engineers and mechanical engineers can qualify for the same jobs too. Aerospace and mechanical engineering curriculums are heavily focused on fluid mechanics (water through pipes or air over wing), solid mechanics (springs under a load), thermodynamics (energy transfer in a steam turbine), and heat transfer (space vehicle heating while entering the atmosphere).

Some curriculums will have mechanical engineers focus more on incompressible fluids (i.e. water). Depending on the school, you will see some give additional emphasis on system dynamics and vibration as well as material science. Aerospace engineers focus more on compressible fluids (i.e. air) and can take undergraduate courses in computational fluid dynamics (CFD). Some schools may offer additional coursework for space applications such as astrodynamics or space vehicle design.

Mechanical engineers arguably have the most diverse job market compared to other engineers. You can find mechanical engineers testing transmissions for automobile manufactures, designing water supply systems for power plants, conducting reliability analysis for machines in paper processing refineries and much more. The majority of aerospace engineers are generally found within the aviation industry as expected. They are involved in designing and testing just about anything on an aircraft such as airfoils or jet engines. Some aerospace engineers have found jobs within the automotive industry to assist in reducing aerodynamic drag on vehicles. The energy industry also has aerospace engineers designing blade profiles for wind turbines. I am sure more jobs exists for aerospace engineers outside of the aviation industry than the few I have mentioned here.

Biological Engineering

Biological engineering is a very interdisciplinary field. These students learn a little bit of solid mechanics, chemistry, biology (obviously), fluids, and electrical engineering. Biological engineering can offer concentrations in biomedical engineering or environmental engineering (sometimes found under civil engineering). Of course, biomedical engineers are taught engineering subjects with applications to human and animal medicine. The environmental engineering concentration focuses on applications to improve environmental quality as well as understanding an industry's impact on public health and the environment.

The biomedical engineering curriculum can contain courses in biomechanics, biomaterials, medical instrumentation and biomedical measurements, and various physiological courses. With the interdisciplinary knowledge, biological engineers devise new methods to diagnose and treat humans and animals such as building new non-invasive imaging devices for doctors. Prosthetics designed by biomedical engineers have come a long way with great leaps in mobility. Some prosthetics are even being design for athletic performance such as those used by athletes in the Paralympics. Pharmaceutical delivery devices are also getting improved by biomedical engineers.

Environmental engineers assist in designing municipal water supplies, wastewater and solid waste treatment systems. Air pollution is a major responsibility to environmental engineers. They build instruments to check air quality as well as devices to filter the air. Often, environmental engineers are some of the first responders to industrial accidents such as the infamous oil spill that occurred in the Gulf of Mexico in 2010

Chemical Engineering

Take any chemical product you use throughout your day – fuel, tires, soap, toothpaste, soda, frozen dinner, plastic bags, vitamins, etc. A chemical engineer had some part in the development of those products. Chemical engineers are the brainiacs of combining system design and economics with chemical processes. They will take small-scale laboratory chemical processes, and turn them into large-scale processes that are quick and affordable. The curriculum for chemical engineering students can entail mass and heat transfer, chemical reaction engineering, process dynamics, polymeric materials, and process economics.

Within manufacturing or petroleum industries, chemical engineers can find themselves as project engineers or design engineers that are in charge of initial design and development of large-scale chemical processing systems. Similar jobs can be found in the pharmaceutical and food industries with a major emphasis on quality control. Poor quality of our society's medicinal drugs and food can have serious repercussions. Energy industries will use chemical engineers to help with pollution control. The agriculture field heavily rely on the chemicals that maximize crop growth. Each one of the industries I've already mentioned also have roles for research and development. Here you can look for ways to tweak some of the known processes or try a totally new chemical process to achieve a better product.

Civil Engineering

Any major structure needed for society such as highways, building, bridges, etc. would be the work of civil engineers. Obviously a big part of their curriculum involves structure mechanics. Some courses in civil engineering could be surveying, construction and material mechanics, engineering hydrology, and geotechnical engineering. Remember that some schools will include environmental engineering within the civil engineering program which will carry over some environmental courses into the program as well.

Skyscrapers, bunkers, and everything in between are constructed with the help of civil engineers. Let's not forget very unique structures such as ocean oil rigs. Civil engineers build and maintain those too. Civil engineers will often work for the government or government contractors since the work involves civilian structures. As mentioned before, civil engineers may be contracted to design and construct highways and interstates as well as bridges across lakes, rivers, canals, and canyons. Around major cities and metropolitan areas, urban planning is a major responsibility for a civil engineer. These engineers will need to consider manipulating heavy traffic flows, available water sources, water distribution and sanitation, and much more.

Electrical/Computer Engineering

Just about every industry utilizes electrical engineers. Try to think of an industry that doesn't use electricity. The electrical engineering curriculum can involve courses in electromagnetics, robotics, power engineering and distribution, RF systems, signal processing, and digital/analog electronics. Some of these classes will also be tied into Computer Engineering programs that may have additional courses such as embedded systems, computer architecture, digital system design, and microprocessor systems design.

An electrical engineer has a part in designing any device that uses electricity and how the device gets electricity. Electrical engineers develop the systems and controls for taking electricity from power plants and distributing it to the community. The robotics industry is heavily supported by electrical engineers. Let's not forget that electrical engineers design radio and satellite communication systems. Computer engineers obviously handle most of the microelectronics and computer component design, but it doesn't just stop there. Some computer engineers go on to work in network architecture and management. Software engineering is another route for computer engineers if they wish to cross over into more computer science based careers.

Industrial Engineering

Industrial engineering is unique from the other disciplines in that people are the main focus of the discipline. Instead of focusing on how a machine or process could operate, industrial engineers are focusing on how people will operate a machine or manipulate a process. Industrial engineers focus on process optimization and management. Courses for an industrial engineering degree can include engineering economics, engineering statistics, ergonomics, and operations and systems design. Industrial engineering is usually for the management focused, but could also fit those who are interested in ergonomics and work environment quality. Some curriculums can contain less high level mathematics or heavy technical subjects in reference to other engineering disciplines, but will have more economical or process management courses. This is not always the case though.

Industrial engineers will often find roles as project engineers or project managers. In this role the industrial engineer's main concern to optimize the team's productivity and manage the project budget. Industrial engineers often study particular manufacturing processes and look for ways to improve the quality of the job or reduce the time required for the job. This could be done by reorganizing the manufacturing process, making a craftsperson's workspace more user friendly, or automate a part of the process. Quality control also falls upon the responsibility of an industrial engineer.

Finding Your Niche

"Your time is limited, so don't waste it living someone else's life. Don't be trapped by dogma - which is living with the results of other people's thinking. Don't let the noise of others' opinions drown out your own inner voice. And most important, have the courage to follow your heart and intuition."

— *Steve Jobs*

What Kind of Engineer Are You?

Now that you have been introduced to the different engineering disciplines, you may be wondering how the heck you are going to pick one. For some of you, it may be pretty obvious which discipline is right for you. Others may find themselves liking more than one or desiring a mixture of the disciplines. There doesn't exist a simple formula such as take the square root of your birth year, add it to the number of letters in your first name, and if that number is even, then you might be a chemical engineer. That would be fascinating if it worked though.

Some choose what engineering discipline they go into by the company they want to work for. Unfortunately, this is not the best approach. Take a company such as Boeing. Although an aerospace company, they also hire mechanical engineers, electrical engineers, computer engineers, industrial engineers, and likely some cross-discipline between those. Setting your vision on a particular company can lead you down a vague path. Some will need more direction than that. Others may look to their hobbies to help them decide on an engineering field such as working on cars or tearing apart computers. This method sounds a little more promising as I assume you do these hobbies because you enjoy them. However, this just answers "What do you currently enjoy doing?" and not "What do you want to do?" Hobbies are a good start, but it can limit you from potential fields of interest.

Another method may be to focus on the curriculum covered in the disciplines. Then ask yourself "What jobs can do I do with that knowledge, and will I enjoy those jobs?" With this approach, you can avoid fields that only have a small number of jobs you would enjoy doing. For example, if you only want to be an aerospace engineer because you want to design rockets, then you may want to research the current and projected job market for such a role. Be sure to pay careful attention to what typical qualifications and desired skills needed for that job. You may find that the job market is very narrow and selective. What happens if you graduate and the rocket industry goes into a slump? If you're laid off or worse, never hired, will you still enjoy other aerospace jobs? Now if you are truly passionate about something that specific, go for it by all means. My point is that having a passion for a job and a passion in a discipline are two different things. If space vehicle design is the only course that sounds interesting out of the 40 class you will take to get a bachelor's degree in aerospace engineering, you may want to look at a different discipline. If you are also interested in aerothermodynamics, aerospace vehicle structure, and propulsion, then aerospace may indeed be the route for you. By choosing an engineering discipline based off what subjects you will be educated in, then you have a higher chance of finding a job you will enjoy and give yourself more opportunities to try different jobs with the same education.

Cross-Disciplines and the Not-So Engineers

Some of you may be worried about not choosing the right discipline. Well you are not stuck with that discipline for life or even throughout college. Many of the classes you take in the first three or four semesters are classes that all engineering students take such as calculus, physics, and chemistry with a few discipline specific courses in between. If you find you don't like those discipline-specific courses (please allow yourself more than one before making this decision), then it's not too late to try another engineering discipline without pushing back your expected graduation date too far. You are probably thinking "Hold on, I don't want to go to school another semester! I would rather stick it out." As expensive as college is, your parents would probably agree with you. However, you should really put this into a different perspective. According to the Bureau of Labor Statistics the average American adult (ages 25 to 54) in 2012 worked more than 8.8 hours a day, slept 7.7 hours, cared for others for 1.2, and did chores for 1.0 hours. How much of their time was spent having fun? Only a measly 2.6 hours a day was spent on leisure and sports. Just under 11% of your time is for fun and over a third of your time is spent working. You are working three times more than you are having fun which is rather depressing. Trust me, if you don't like your job, the 8.8 hours will feel like 20 hours. Let's say you picked the perfect engineering discipline and got the job you dreamed about though. That would practically turn the 8.8 hours of work into leisure (now making a total of 11.4 hours or fun), and you are having fun roughly half of your day. Would pushing back graduation to gain that extra enjoyment out of your work and life be worth it? I think the choice is obvious.

Money still may be an issue when considering switching engineering disciplines and pushing back your graduation. At the end of the 2011 – 2012 academic year, the average annual cost of tuition, room, and board at a public school was $14,300 according to the National Center for Education

Statistics. Let's say you are considering switching to a different engineering field, and the switch would push your graduation back two years costing an additional $28,600. You could buy a new car with that kind of cash. What you need to account for is that starting salaries for engineers range from $50,000 to $80,000 on average (depending on company, location, engineering discipline, etc.). You could pay off that $28,600 loan in very little time with a salary of that size as long as you avoid big purchases such as cars or houses. You will need to build up credit for those big purchases anyways and paying off a loan of that size helps. Pushing back graduation is obviously not ideal, but very do-able.

Before switching to a different engineering discipline, you should talk to an advisor of the new discipline to make sure it is what you expect. If you are not thinking about switching, I still highly encourage you to take a course that is out of your discipline, especially if it counts towards an elective credit. Taking courses in other engineering disciplines help justify that you are in the right discipline, or introduce you to how fun things can be in a different field. A little bit of knowledge in other engineering disciplines can really boost your career as well. In fact, many engineers can and will be challenged with problems outside of their engineering education. A good example would be the mechanical engineers that are responsible for testing combustion engines. There is a lot of measurement instrumentation such as thermocouples and pressure probes that need to be wired to signal conditions, data acquisition systems, and system networks. Then the programming for the data analysis needs to be done. A little knowledge in electrical engineering and computer science can really make life easier for these engineers. Cross-disciplined engineers are coming a hot commodity amongst the industry because of the versatility they provide.

You are also not stuck being an engineer for the rest of your life. Many engineers go on to be educators, managers, medical doctors, and even lawyers. Switching professions mid-career is quite a common practice amongst engineers. They are not switching because they don't enjoy engineering anymore. They are switching because the engineer inside of them makes them naturally curious to try new things. You should never be afraid to try out other disciplines and job roles when you get the opportunity in the future.

Is Engineering For You?
If you have gone through high school remaining somewhere near the top of your class, chances are you have been told that you should become a doctor, lawyer, or engineer. I personally like the idea of smart kids going into engineering considering they will be the workforce that designs

planes and nuclear power plants. However, being the smart kid in high school does not obligate you to be an engineer. I have witnessed some of the brightest students become disgusted with engineering after only a few semesters. They weren't disgusted because engineering was too hard. They just thought engineering was about as enjoyable as licking sandpaper.

The reverse can also be said. If you radiate mediocrity, you are not banned from engineering either. I would hate to know how many students never considered engineering because someone did not mention it to them. There have been hordes of students considered "average" before college, but went on to thrive in engineering schools and their careers. Mediocrity is often stemmed by lack of motivation due to lack of interest. The unique topics in engineering can kindle a student into success.

You should not feel like you must go to a school such as the prestigious MIT or Stanford to be a successful engineer. There is no doubt that these schools recruit some of the best minds in the nation. However, this does not mean they produce some of the best engineers. In Malcolm Gladwell's *David and Goliath*, Caroline Sacks is a bright student fascinated by biology that faces a decision to go to the elite Brown University or the relatively subparUniversity of Maryland. In the end, she chose Brown which is probably the obvious choice for most. However, she gradually became overwhelmed at the fact that she was no longer THE smart person in the class because so was everyone else. This led to a major lack of confidence, poor grades, and eventually led her to switching to a non-science major. When looking back at her decision of going to Brown over the University of Maryland, she says, "If I had gone to the University of Maryland, I would still be in science."

Malcolm Gladwell uses this example as a classic case of taking the jump from big fish in a small pond to a small fish in a big pond. Some will suggest that the small pond is better and others will argue that the large pond is better. I only mean to add that the better pond is the one you feel comfortable in and thrive in. Do not be scared that you will miss out on your dream job because you didn't go to an elite school. Companies across the nation are starting to realize that students graduating from elite schools are not that drastically different from students that graduate from average schools. For most cases, the top students from elite colleges and average colleges show very little difference in their job performance.

Learning to Fail

You are probably thinking "Fail?! I'm not supposed to fail anything!" I am not saying that you will fail, but you should consider that the academic difficulty is going to increase significantly when you go into an engineering program. Also consider what actually defines failure for you. Is it receiving an F? Maybe failing is really getting a C. What if the entire class got an A, but you got the lonely B. That is still a respectable performance, but you have likely placed your rank at the bottom of the class. This can do some serious work on your ego and motivation. As I mentioned earlier, the typical students that are encouraged to go into engineering are those who have remained at the top of their class practically their whole lives. Failure is not something these students face on a regular basis if at all.

If you look up retention rates for college freshmen in engineering, you can find numbers ranging from 30% to 70% depending on the school. That means a large chunk of the new engineering students have transferred to a different major outside engineering or completely dropped out of college. Apart from engineering truly not fitting into a student's interest, what is going on to cause all of these students to quit engineering? A large portion of those transfers can be accredited to the students experiencing failure for the first time. However, the students are not failing in terms of grades. Most of those kids are not receiving F's for that matter. They are getting grades of D's and C's. Giving one of these college students a C in the first semester can be the equivalent to telling a high school superstar that they were never really that special. This can be a huge shot to the student's ego and plummet their motivation.

So what can we do to make engineering education less overwhelming? One wrong answer is to make the curriculum easier. Regardless if we expect a little or a lot from engineering students, the engineering principles do not change. There is just a certain amount of knowledge we must know to become adequate engineers. Having less educated engineers to build bridges and cars would result in a catastrophe. Not only can we not make the engineering curriculum easier, but the necessary competency of an engineer is raised all the time as our society gets more and more advanced. Imagine taking a present day senior engineering student on a trip back in time to visit Isaac Newton or Leonardo da Vinci. Both of these guys are considered geniuses by today's society. However, the technology those geniuses had available would be quite archaic compared to what our senior engineering student is accustomed to having. When our student shows those two how a smartphone worked, their minds would be blown. Trying to make the curriculum easier on students when in reality the sciences are getting more involved and complicated is not the solution.

One method of raising the retention rate could be to prepare students to handle failure instead of letting them believe that failure is unacceptable. This responsibility falls just as much on the student as it is does the educators however. You need to have *sisu*. Although sisu has been interpreted in different ways, the Finnish term stands for resilience and grit. You should be able to grit out failure and learn from it. Sticking out hardship and failure can be quite enlightening, after the initial sickening feeling that is. Failure can be quite an impactful form of learning. The emotional response tied with a lesson to change your method will stick with you the rest of your life. I can still remember tests that I took years ago and pinpoint exactly where I went wrong on some of the simplest problems (always remember to carry the negative sign). How else do we know not to stick objects into power outlets anymore? Once you have this ability, there is very little that could stop you from becoming a world class engineer.

Being able to accept failure, also comes with throwing out your pride. You should be proud of what you are capable of doing, but do not let it prevent you from learning more. When the professor lectures and you have no idea what he is talking about, raise your hand and ask. Forget about the opinions of other students and even your professor's opinion of you if you feel your questions are dumb. After you do this once or twice and you get the information you were looking for, asking 'dumb' questions becomes exponentially easier to do, and you won't be afraid to do it again and again. If you are not getting the 'eureka' moment still, see about getting your smart friend in class to help you out or search online. Oh yeah, get a smart friend. Every engineer should have one. Use every method you have available to overcome. Lectures notes and textbooks are no longer the only source of information. We now have access to open courseware lectures online with really great professors and YouTube videos full of tutorials. I understand the desire of being respected for your intelligence, but you don't earn that by not asking questions or refusing to accept you don't know everything. You earn that respect by doing well on your exams, especially after you bombed the previous one. Everyone will take the bombed test as a fluke when you ace the following test. So swallow your pride. Allow failure to be the biggest motivator and educator. Success will follow.

So far I have approached failure as an expectation that it may occur only a handful of times. What about when you are constantly failing? When should you throw in the towel? Unfortunately, I cannot provide you a straightforward answer. I can give you my opinion on a few considerations before giving up and jumping ship to a different major. Students will give up too often because they were having trouble in only one class. If this is the case for you, do not give up. I'll share a little secret. Some schools will have what are called "weed out" classes. Although it may not be the school's intention, usually one or two classes are going to challenge you way more than others and weed out the students that can't make it. Often these classes are one of the engineering fundamentals classes such thermodynamics, fluids, physics, etc. These courses can be tough by design because everything you are presented in your engineering courses will require a solid foundation in those fundamentals. You can find a way to get through a class or two even if you receive a C or D. You GPA won't suffer too badly from one or two C's or D's as long as you have plenty of A's to keep it high. Your undesirable grade does not directly correlate with the knowledge you gained from the course and your ability to succeed afterwards.

However, if you are consistently struggling in multiple classes in the same semester (3 or more), or you are just barely passing one or two classes for a series of semesters, reconsidering engineering as your career choice may be a legitimate decision. There is no shame in trying engineering and learning it wasn't for you. Switching out of engineering does not mean you are dumb by any measure. Society needs intelligent and capable people in plenty of other jobs such as meteorologists, journalists, and even business entrepreneurs. In fact, most of the engineers I know would be terrible at other jobs. The decision to leave engineering is ultimately yours to make. Before you do, make sure it is not over one or two classes. Also devise a plan of what major you plan to conquer next before dropping your engineering classes. Do not drop out due to frustration without thinking about what you are going to do next. Be logical and think clearly when you make decisions like this. You should feel accomplished for just trying engineering. Many people would never consider it. Just as I mentioned earlier, take the disappointment of failure, and use that to motivate you to accomplish your new endeavor.

Have an End-Goal

"We are the creative force of our life, and through our own decisions rather than our conditions, if we carefully learn to do certain things, we can accomplish those goals.

– Stephen Covey

Stephen Covey's *The 7 Habits of Highly Effective People* has sold over 15 million copies since its publication in 1989. The second habit of the seven is "begin with the end in mind". In other words, take your first steps in the most straight forward path towards your final goal, not just in the general direction. It occurs quite often in college that someone changes their final goal once, twice, or maybe 20 times. Since this is a book for engineering students, I am going to assume you are going to at least stay in engineering in regards to changing your major. However, your end-goal should not be what you want a bachelor's degree in. Your end-goal is what you want to do right after your bachelor's degree. For most students, you will want a decent paying job that is semi-close to your hometown or on the other side of the world. Others may consider doing research, getting published, and receiving a masters or PhD at the same school or another school. Some overachievers will do both! Whichever your destination may become, I want to share with you the typical options, a few hints, and some strategies that you can use to better align yourself with your end-goal in mind. You may already know what you want, but I highly suggest that you look over all the options I mention as you will be surprised at what could intrigue you.

Full-Time Job

Like I mentioned earlier, the majority of students are just looking for an enjoyable, decent paying job right after they graduate. Heck, that's why you went to college! Well there are some interesting things that occur within the engineering field in regards to getting a full-time job. To start with, engineering students are getting recruited well before graduation. I have personally known several students that had full-time job offers in October although they didn't graduate until to the following May. The offer was contingent on their graduation, but that is still a full seven months before the student's earliest start date. I'm sure there have been many students before that have received much earlier offers.

Let's look at the timeline a little more. Most colleges will have their largest career fair during the fall semester. In other words, the fall semester is usually the best opportunity to meet the most employers, so be ready for it. Now what will you have to offer the recruiters come the fall of your senior year? If you interview for a job seven months before you graduate, you are going into that interview with only the accomplishments you have achieved through your junior year. That is, you are showing the recruiters a resume with a GPA that will not include the grades from some of your toughest classes that a student typically takes in the last year. Not a bad deal huh? You have to look at the flip-side of this though. Waiting until your senior year to pull up your GPA or start getting involved in extracurricular activities may be too late, but do not let that stop you from trying. Senior year can also include projects that make for a great way to sell your skills and experience with hard technical objectives. Let's say you don't get a job in the fall semester though. That's OK. Don't freak out. Employers still recruit in the spring.

Also, there are many occasions when companies want a little more isolation with the students that a career fair cannot offer. These companies will host their own recruiting sessions on campus in which they will invite certain majors to join in to hear about the company and available employment opportunities. This is often the best time to really sell yourself to the company in hopes for an interview. By going to these sessions, it shows you are more interested in these particular companies relative to the numerous other companies that only go to the career fair. Also, it gives you a chance to present yourself casually to a recruiter (no suit and tie needed). You will be more confident than you would be in a career fair environment just by dressing casually. However, leave the lazy classroom apparel of wrinkled, gym clothes at home. In college, you will learn that free stuff is some of the best stuff. More often than not, these companies also provide free food and drinks which makes it worthwhile to go whether you are interested in the company or not. If you do go for more than just free pizza, ask questions and be sure to network with the recruiters after they give their spill of the company. Get business cards from them if they have any, and give them your résumé. These sessions may be followed up with the recruiters asking you to have a casual dinner with them the next day or arranging a time for an interview. Went for the pizza and left with an interview – talk about winning the day!

Now there are some interesting things you need to know about how companies recruit. A stigma exists about some big name companies' practice of only recruiting from particular elite schools. While this isn't totally a myth, it does not happen as much you think. Most companies actually recruit locally, since the travel for the recruiters is cheaper. Even big name companies such as General Electric or Siemens recruit locally. They have locations all over world, but they still go the schools that are local to their offices. So do not feel as if you have to go to MIT to work for NASA. I'm sure NASA would be glad to have an MIT applicant, but they also recruit from middle of the pack colleges.

Actually, there has been a lot of money spent on research as to which colleges produce the best graduates. The answer? **All of them**. Previously, I gave brief description of Caroline Sacks's story from *David and Goliath* in reference to choosing what school to choose. The author of *David and Goliath*, Malcolm Gladwell, further iterates on this big fish, small pond scenario. He compares the top economics graduate students from the elite schools of Harvard, MIT, Yale, Princeton, Columbia, Stanford, and Chicago to the non-elite schools of Boston University, University of Toronto, and other non-top 30 schools. Shockingly, the top percent from the elite schools and non-elite schools performed at the same level! This result is the case for most college majors, and the industry is starting to become aware of it. So do not feel as if you are at a disadvantage because of what school you go to. As long as you are at the top of your class, you can be compete with the best of them.

An important thing to know as an engineer is how big the co-operative (co-op) education program is at your school. I say 'big', but really what I mean is that you should research how many students within your engineering major actively participate in the co-op program. This information is usually recorded on a regular basis by the school's career services. If it becomes difficult to find, then it might be safe to assume the program is not very big. You should know about the school's co-op program not only so you can participate (further described in Chapter 6), but also to build an idea of the competition you will have when it comes time for full-time job interviews. Let's say 50% of mechanical engineers participate in a school's co-op program. If you are a mechanical engineer, this roughly means that half of the graduating seniors of your class will already have at least a year of experience when they apply for full-time jobs. This is huge advantage! If a school has constantly supplied their common recruiters with experienced co-op students, then it is possible that the recruiters may come to expect that co-op experience from their pool of prospects. I supply a pretty good argument for participating in a co-op program in chapter 6, but it is not critical to get a full-time job. Remember that this is a major-specific issue. For example, a large percentage of mechanical engineers that have co-op experience will not really affect the competition of electrical engineers. Just be ready to compete with the best in your class.

Graduate School

Some students will know from the beginning that the academia world is for them. Others will figure it out along the way and few more will go into graduate school just because they didn't find a job right after getting their bachelor's degree. Whichever your pathway is to get there, going to graduate school is a great decision. As more and more schools are pumping out fresh engineers with bachelor's degrees, graduate degrees are the next best thing to springboard your career ahead of the rest in industry as well as academia. Of course, there is the decision of choosing a masters or doctoral program.

A master's degree program varies in the requirements. It can take anywhere between 1 and a half to 2 years on average to complete. Typically, there is a thesis or non-thesis route. I highly recommend doing a thesis route if it's available. It may seem overwhelming that you have to publish a highly technical thesis for the world to scrutinize during the time you are also taking high level graduate courses, but the satisfaction is well worth the effort. You would not take the same number of courses per semester as you did during your undergraduate career. A full-time graduate student will usually take a maximum of three courses a semester and eventually taper off to only one or two courses a semester. Plus, a thesis route is arguably the same amount of effort as a non-thesis route. A non-thesis route will usually require taking more classes than the thesis route plus a high-level project or comprehensive exam. For engineers who are already at a full-time job and wanting to take a master's program part-time, a non-thesis route may be more favorable as you may not have the time to do research but enough time to take one class a semester.

PhD programs are the next step to into elite academia. Some schools offer direct admission from a bachelor's degree and some will require you to start on a master's degree track before progressing towards a PhD. Most students complete PhD programs in 4 to 5 years. This seems like a long time, but there is a lot to complete. Doctoral students will usually be required to take qualifying exams, *quals* for short, during their first two or three semesters as a PhD candidate. Qualifying exams cover topics you were taught during your undergraduate education. Unfortunately for most students, about 2 or 3 years have passed since a student has taken those courses, and they may be a little rusty on the topics. Most engineering quals are divided into three sections with math being one of three. The others will be of your choosing, depending on your major. So for mechanical engineering PhD students, they could take a mathematics section, fluid dynamics section, and thermodynamics section. Quals are given in different fashions depending on the school, but the two methods are usually given as oral exams or written exams. Instead of receiving a grade such as an A or B, these exams are simply pass or fail. Don't worry. Most schools give you an opportunity to retake the quals if you needed. After getting completely stressed out by quals, PhD students still face delivering a dissertation proposal, writing a dissertation, and defending their dissertation. A dissertation is practically a much longer, more in-depth thesis that includes research you have done as a student. It is also fairly common of PhD students to submit multiple research articles into academic journals with most of the research being the same of that included in the student's dissertation.

After thinking graduate school is your next step, you need to know how to get in. To get into an undergraduate program, you will need to take the ACT or SAT. If you have already taken this, you probably remember how much you enjoyed that! Yes, that's sarcasm at its finest. Well for graduate school, you will need to take the Graduate Record Exam or GRE. This test is currently scored from 130 to 170 (ever wonder what was wrong with the 0 – 100 system?) and contains three sections: Verbal Reasoning, Quantitative Reasoning, and Analytical Writing (scored 0 - 6). More information can be found at www.ets.org/gre. For engineering graduate school, you will really want to focus on the Quantitative Reasoning section. This is where you get to put to mathematical and analytical skills to work. You really won't need the advanced math and engineering topics covered in college. Most of the math on the test is arithmetic, algebra, and geometry. The questions will not be straightforward though such as being told to use the quadratic formula to solve a binomial. Many of the problems will require to you come up with your own solution method instead. You could be asked to figure out how many different 5 characters passwords could be formed using 0-9 as the first two characters and any letter of the alphabet for the last three characters as long as only even numbers are used and no character is repeated. This is a simple example, but you get the idea of how the questions will be asked. Be aware of a slight twist to this computer based test – its adaptive. The verbal reasoning and quantitative reasoning are split into two halves each. The second half will be more difficult if you do well on the first half. You want this to happen! A higher difficulty on second half gives you the chance to score higher on the test. Opposite to this, if you do poorly on the first half, the second half will have a lower difficulty. Unfortunately, even if you get the same amount of total questions correct as someone with a more difficult 2nd half, your score is likely to be lower. Some schools take the GRE score as a sanity check and some schools are quite serious about its weight on your admission consideration. I suggest you contact your graduate coordinator at your prospective school and ask how they perceive these scores. Unfortunately, schools will not publish a minimum required score for admission. Most schools will publish the average score of the students admitted, which gives you a good baseline. Students vary in how much they should study for this exam. At a minimum, you should work through an entire practice test to understand the style of questions to expect. Plenty of study guides are available and worth the money, so don't be shy to spend a little cash on them. You can schedule the test ahead of time to give yourself a deadline to be ready (this can be helpful in motivating yourself to study). The test is easy to schedule since it is computer based and available at most college campuses.

Most students come out of their bachelor's degree poor and in debt. So why would they want to continue this trend into graduate school? Well, graduate schools can offer a few financial options that were not available to you as an undergraduate. Assistantships are the most common method for a graduate student to pay for school. An assistantship differs from a scholarship in that you usually agree to work for the school instead of just keeping a certain GPA (graduate schools usually have their own policy on GPA regardless if you have an assistantship). The work you will be doing for the school can differ however. A teaching assistantship will require you to teach a fundamentals course or lab. Research assistantships are another option. These will require you to work under a faculty member to help in some form of research. Generally, the research you are assisting with can be what you use for a thesis or dissertation. This is the favorable deal in my opinion. Regardless of which assistantship you get, the normal deal is that you have to work 20 hours a week. In return, a large portion, if not all, of your tuition can be paid for by the school, and then you can still receive a monthly stipend that is usually just enough to cover all your bills, groceries, etc.

Graduate research fellowships are another way to get money for graduate school. These come from private industry and government entities with the National Science Foundation being one of the largest providers of fellowships. To keep things simple, the money for fellowships is set aside when a group such as the NSF decides that advancement is needed on a particular topic. The topics can be quite specific and also very general. Then you write a proposal for research that you could do for that particular topic. If your proposal is deemed worthy enough, they offer you the fellowship. In return, there is usually terms of conditions of what the funding body expects from your research. The amount of fellowship money can vary from a few thousand for one year to several thousand over several years. The available fellowships are typically well advertised since people want someone to be doing the research, so a few minutes of internet surfing can help you further understand what is available.

Other Options

There are countless students who go through the entire engineering curriculum just to realize they don't really want to be an engineer. Some even knew they didn't want to be an engineer from the beginning, but they went through the engineering education regardless. Why torture yourself with all those hard classes to receive a degree in something you don't want to do? Because engineering is a great stepping stone to very lucrative professions that don't require a specific undergraduate degree.

A good example is a student who desires to go to medical school. Engineering is a great stepping stone into medical school, especially biomedical engineering. However, biomedical engineers are not accepted just because of their major. Medical school requires a certain level of work ethic and technical rigor that is comparable to the engineering curriculum. To put this bluntly, a biomedical engineer or even an electrical engineer with a 3.7 GPA trumps a fine arts major with a 3.7 GPA. Before taking the medical school entrance exam, MCAT, you will need to take certain pre-med courses in math, biology, chemistry, physics, and English. The required classes can differ depending on the medical school you would apply to. Not many curriculums contain all of the pre-med classes needed for taking the MCAT, but engineering curriculums contain most of them. Admission to medical school doesn't just stop at major, GPA, and MCAT scores. Extracurricular activities, work experience, and experience around a medical practice also helps. If you decide medical school might be a good choice for you, be sure to talk with a pre-med representative at your school so that you can take all the right classes.

On another part of the spectrum is the option of going into law school. Intellectual property, IP, has been a major issue ever since the beginning of war, and everybody wanted to have the best weapons. Maintaining justice amongst intellectual property such as patents, source code, etc. is a major concern for any company or innovator. In fact, there has been a recent battle between Samsung and Apple over a few patents that value upwards to millions of dollars. Lawyers with political science backgrounds do their best to keep up with the technological advances, but many times it requires a technical background to understand differences between patents and how to recognize patent fraud. Cue the engineer to go to law school to make some serious cash in IP law.

If medical school or law school doesn't sound appealing, there is still yet another option - military officer. The military offers great opportunities for engineering graduates in the Air Force, Army, Navy, and Marine Corps. The military might seem a little extreme for someone considering an engineering degree, but think about these names before you make any rash judgment: Buzz Aldrin and Neil Armstrong. These are two of the most notable astronauts, military pilots, AND engineers. Buzz received a mechanical engineering degree from West Point (after turning down a full ride to MIT), and Neil got an aerospace engineering degree from Purdue. Still think the military is a crazy option for an engineer? Within the military, you can often use your technical education as a research or project officer, or you could do something completely different such as mission command. Having an engineering degree can help you have a competitive edge for the lucrative military jobs everyone wants, i.e. pilot. Military services also offer incentives such as paying back your student loans. Continuing education is a great value to the military, so they also support you continuing in graduate level degrees if you desire. On many occasions the military will pay for it too! Techies need to face facts. The military has all the coolest toys. Designing the toys is one thing, but playing with them is a whole other level of fun. For non-techies, the military can supply you an outlet to still use your degree and become a leader in a noble profession. If you are intrigued by these options, I encourage you to look online, talk to recruiting officers, and gather all the information you can.

Surviving the Engineering Student Life

"The scientists of today think deeply instead of clearly. One must be sane to think clearly, but one can think deeply and be quite insane."

— *Nikola Tesla*

There is no questioning how crazy the life of an engineering student can be. In 2011, a study has found that senior engineering students study 19 hours a week on average according to the National Survey of Student Engagement. That time is in addition to the 15 – 20 hours a week they spend inside the classroom and labs, which practically makes it a full-time job they are paying for instead of getting paid. I'm here to tell you that it is more than possible to succeed as an engineer without giving up all your free-time and going insane. Nevertheless, a high level of commitment and time management coupled with a few tricks of the trade is necessary to come out on top of your engineering class.

In this chapter, I will go over a few strategies for studying, optimizing your learning efforts, and obtaining a proper balance of the work hard, play hard lifestyle. Some of the suggestions are solely from the author's opinion, and others are backed up by scientific data. If you were to take anything away from this chapter, remember that you need to <u>find what works best for you</u>. Your best strategy may be a combination of the ones below, or it could be one that isn't mentioned at all. As a future engineer, the best way to find out is to experiment with them all.

Learning How to Study

Most high school students are never really taught how they should study. They are just told to study which eventually leads them to just rereading the material (time-consuming) or making note cards (not as effective as you think). Most kids in the top of their high school class are gifted enough that don't really have to study much anyways. Remember, these are also the kids that will likely consider being an engineer. Those of you who got through high school easily without studying a bit, this is my attempt to warn you that you will not likely get away with that in college. As an embarrassing example, I never considered studying throughout high school and my first few semesters in college. I did most of my homework during class, and then never looked at the material again. Then thermodynamics came, and I earned the high mark of a 51 out of 100 on my first test. I thought my professor was joking, and I even laughed when he handed it to me... It turns out he wasn't. Brushing it off as a fluke, I approached the next test the same way as I have done before. The result – 53. This is when it finally clicked that I needed to study. The only problem was that I wasn't sure how, so I tried every way imaginable. I even tried memorizing study guides while under water after watching some guy on TV do it with a deck of cards. While that method is not listed below, I have listed some that I found worked best for me. So please consider some of the methods before you figure it out the hard way. If you do make it to the top of your engineering class without studying, then feel free to share your secret with me, and I'll make you a co-author on my next book.

Learn by Teaching

Go ahead and search the internet for the phase "Learn by Teaching", and countless links will come up. This is a strategy that has been proven over and over to be an impactful method of learning. The key factor in this method is that it forces you to arrange ideas in simple terms. This method also brings out what you do not know instead of testing you on what you already do know (there is a difference). One of the many quotes that the rock star physicist Albert Einstein gave to world is "If you can't explain it to a six year old, you don't understand it yourself." In fact, another Nobel Prize winning physicist Richard Feynman was known for applying this teaching method to help himself learn any topic. His lectures on all levels of physics are world renown for their simplicity with his ability to put things into layman's terms which demonstrates his practice with the method. I will break down a process similar to his so that you can become the next Feynman. If you do become the next Nobel laureate after reading this book, you at least owe me a high-five.

Step 1: Take out one sheet of notebook paper and write the topic you plan to teach yourself or someone else at the top of the page.

Step 2: Using only one side of the sheet of paper, start writing down the simplest explanation that any non-engineer could understand. Avoid using any heavy, technical jargon that you would use to show off your mental muscle. Use hand drawn pictures as needed, but keep the sketches simples. The sketches need to legible by anyone. You will be surprised by how simple hand-drawn figures stick in your memory.

Step 3: As you progress through the six-year-old level explanation, you will soon notice any fuzzy areas that you don't fully understand. Don't be discouraged. Finding those fuzzy areas was the point of the exercise. Go back to your class notes or textbook to review the missing pieces until you can write a clear explanation.

Step 4: If you need more than one side of a piece of paper, your topic is too complex. Break it down further into smaller topics with each topic having its own sheet.

The DIY Study Guide

Creating your own study guide can be extremely helpful in the initial approach to studying. By creating your own study guide, you are defining what material will be covered on the exam and predicting what a professor is more likely to focus on. Some students that have had the professor before can usually give you an idea of what material could be on the test. This could seriously help your prediction of the material. Don't be afraid to ask the professor either. They are not the scary, sociopaths that we think they are (well most of them are not), and they can be straightforward with you most of the time. Having a clear range of the material covered gives you a starting line. You could do this by first creating an outline to the lecture notes or taking the textbook chapters and subchapters as the start to your outline. This should give you a high level overview of the material and how it interconnects. It may be obvious that you do not remember some parts of your personal outline. This should raise a flag as a place to focus on and use the learn-by-teaching technique mentioned above.

Don't Reinvent the Wheel

If you are still having trouble understanding a certain problem, there is a pretty good chance you can find a solution to a similar problem via the internet. Of course, I am in no way suggesting that you break any honor code or plagiarize someone else's work. Universities are very serious about this and can expel you for it. With that said, you should still consider using every available resource that's legal. You should be able to find worked examples all over YouTube, forums, and Wikipedia. Somebody has worked hard to solve a similar problem before, and you should capitalize on the opportunity if they were nice enough to explain it to the public.

Study Groups vs Going Solo

Study groups can be helpful. Other opinions in the group can shed light on topics that you are a little confused on. It also gives you an opportunity to test out the learn-by-teaching method described earlier. However, you should be cautious of who you choose to study with. Typically, students always choose their friends to study with. This makes complete sense on a social level, but maybe not so much on an academic level. You should remember that you are more likely to get off topic and really distracted when you are around your friends. There is a reason you are friends, and that reason probably isn't your shared passion for engineering. These friends can easily get you distracted from studying. If you and your friend do actually share an engineering passion, then look no further for a study partner. Other dangers of study groups exist such as fear of embarrassment over not being as knowledgeable as the group. This could lead you to neglect the material you actually need to focus on and only discussing the material you do know to avoid feeling uncomfortable. If you choose to study with a group, be sure to study with someone who can keep you on track.

Studying solo can be less distracting and more similar to the test-taking environment. Studying alone also allows you to use the strategies that work for you. If you end up needing help, then your smart friend is only a phone call or text message away (I wouldn't suggest trying a dumb friend). Don't worry. I'm not trying to convince you that you must lock yourself away in a dungeon until you can recite everything in fluid mechanics in Latin. Although that would be quite impressive, I'm merely suggesting that you study by yourself for a short period before studying with others. Then you can bring some knowledge to the table if anyone else needs help and solidify that knowledge by teaching it to others.

Work Hard, Play Hard

Just as important as studying is doing the exact opposite. You need to go have fun. There is a cliché saying that "college will be the best years of your life." While, I don't exactly agree, simply on the account that there are still great things in life after college, college is still a prime time to have fun. If you spend your entire four years of college with your face in the books (five years for those who take a 'victory lap'), there is a high risk that college will actually be the worst years of your life. It is actually quite beneficial to your learning that you stop trying to do it all the time. Think of your brain as a muscle. You can only work it so much before little to no improvement occurs. This is the perfect time to get engineering off your mind. Go outside and throw the Frisbee with a friend. Try out the new restaurant in town. If you are of age, you deserve a drink for your hard work. It's okay to reward yourself. Actually, it's beneficial to reward yourself.

Some of the fun ideas I mentioned above require more than just yourself. Even the most stereotypical engineers have friends. The more friends, the better. That probably seems like something your mother would say. However, I am suggesting you go out with friends for a different reason. You need to learn to network. Other than stand-out grades and engineering experience, networking is possibly the heaviest influence on a college student's chance at getting a job. Not just a job right after college, but it could also help you move your career somewhere else 5 or 10 years down the road. The friends you make in college will work in companies all over the world. Some may start their own company. They could be just the person to call when you are ready to change jobs as they could provide a great recommendation to their boss or your friend could even be the boss.

On top of the networking advantage, being social keeps you fresh on your soft skills such as conversation and body language. These skills can make or break an interview. If you are not practiced with conversing with a complete stranger, how do you expect to be 'buddy-buddy' come the time for an interview and that stranger now has the power to grant you a great job. Want to know a great and fun way to get practice talking to strangers? Just walk up to one, and say "Hi!" Waiters and waitresses do this all the time. Busting their butts waiting tables isn't just helping them pay for college. Those working students are learning valuable social skills. Walking up to a complete stranger may seem a little too bold for some. A good way around that is to grab some of your friends and make a game out of setting each other up. For example, in the TV series *How I Met Your Mother*, the bro of all TV bro's, Barney, plays a game called "Have you met Ted?" The rules were simple. Barney would inconspicuously bring his friend Ted within an arm's reach of a complete stranger which was usually a pretty girl. As he tapped the stranger on the shoulder, he would simply say to them "Have you met Ted?", and then walk away with Ted stranded to start a conversation. Doing this trick on your friends is not only hilarious, but will get them comfortable with starting a conversation on the fly with a complete stranger.

Strong Body, Strong Mind

"Physical fitness is not only one of the most important keys to a healthy body, it is the basis of dynamic and creative intellectual activity."

— *John F. Kennedy*

Every Engineer Should Exercise

There is no doubt that a strong link exists between intellectual performance and physical fitness. I have experienced this first hand, watched others gain similar benefits, as well as read research that has consistently proven the correlation. I am not saying you should simultaneously study transport phenomena during a 5 mile run on the treadmill. Although this happens to be a very common scene at university gyms, studying during exercise has actually shown to be quite ineffective and lead to rather embarrassing falls on the treadmill in front of everyone to see. The consistent pursuit of studying following exercise is the key.

When you exercise, a variety of chemicals is produced in the brain such as the ever popular endorphins serotonin and dopamine. Brain derived neurotrophic factor (BDNF) and the hormone Insulin Growth Factor 1 (IGF-1) are some lesser known but just as important chemicals also produced in the brain during exercise. Essentially, you create a chemical cocktail that primes your brain for learning RIGHT AFTER exercise. That's right. Instead of that morning coffee right before class, you could go on a quick run right before and be more alert, attentive, and able to remember more from the lecture. When you drink your coffee in the morning, the caffeine in coffee stimulates the body to produce epinephrine (better known as adrenaline). Well, your body can produce epinephrine without coffee by stimulating it with a higher heart rate. We all love caffeine, and it is hard to give up. Well I'm not saying you should give up coffee; it does have health benefits such as providing you with antioxidants. Just don't overdo it. Caffeinated drinks can send you into an energy crash after the effects wear off. You may be motivated during your caffeine buzz, but you will only be thinking about a nap when it wears off. Exercise's stimulant effect can last for longer periods than those produced by caffeine alone and doesn't come with that heavy crash effect. For college students, grabbing a small coffee at your local café can really add up in cost and calories, especially with you load it with cream and sugar. Talk about a way to save you money and burn some calories just by trading coffee for exercise.

In the book *Spark: The Revolutionary New Science of Exercise and The Brain*, John J. Ratey describes how Naperville Central High School took average eighth graders and created an academic global powerhouse that finished 6th in math and 1st in science on the TIMSS (Trends in International Mathematics and Science Study). Those kids were competing with Japan and Singapore who have continued to lead the world in academics. So what changed them so drastically? They adopted a new physical education class that emphasized aerobic activities first thing in the morning before the normal school classes. Later in the book, Ratey explains that "exercise improves learning on three levels: first, it optimizes your mind-set to improve alertness, attention, and motivation; second, it prepares and encourages nerve cell to bind to one another, which is the cellular basis to log new information; and third, it spurs new development of nerve cells from stem cells in the hippocampus." This combination prepares your brain to absorb whatever knowledge is thrown at it.

So you are not a morning person? Neither is most of the student population. The good thing is that the effects of exercise on learning can work at later parts in the days. Remember, it is the relationship of the time between exercising and studying that is important. The morning is just more effective since your classes are typically offered in the first half of the day. However, feel free to experiment with exercising in the afternoon and then studying afterwards. Afternoon exercise is potentially the best stress reliever, and it sets you up for a great night of sleep. Imagine being stuck inside a classroom and/or lab all day. Pushing some weights around or putting some miles on your shoes is a great way to get you out of that brain-numbing sensation you can get from getting pummeled with theories and computations all day.

Exercise is one of the most underrated forms of optimizing your learning potential. You don't have to be previous athlete to start. Even just a little helps and goes a long way. Simply just find something you enjoy doing so that you know you can sustain the healthy habit. Let's not forget that there is always health for an additional good reason to do it. While we are being honest, let's talk about the other elephant in the room involving exercise. Being fit is attractive, and your college years is a great time to be attractive. Just picture yourself being approached by an attractive person that asks you if you study Kinesiology or play a college sport, and then you get to respond with "Actually, I'm an engineer."

Sleep is a Necessity, Not an Option

A typical scene in the engineering student world is a student gazing over textbooks at 4am in order to cram for a test that starts at 8am. This doesn't just happen once, but can be a weekly occurrence or even daily towards the end of the semester to prepare for finals. Some may think this is inevitable when preparing for a big exam. I am here to tell you that trading more study time for less sleep is absolutely one of the most inefficient methods of studying or doing anything intellectual for that matter. Then again, if you are wanting the half-dead, pale skin and irritated, red-eye appearance to audition for the role of Zombie-4 in the next episode of *The Walking Dead*, studying all night is just for you.

Nikola Tesla produced approximately 280 patents, practically developed the basis of alternating current electronics, and is arguably one of the best engineers to ever live. When you get a unit of measurement named after you (magnetic fields are measured in Tesla), it's likely you are a big deal. What is not commonly known is that Tesla constantly pushed himself through his work and refused to sleep. There were many spans when he would only average 4 hours of sleep or less every night. Eventually, he was hospitalized on more than one occasion because of this habit.

You do not have to skip on sleep to be as accomplished as Tesla. Lack of sleep will actually make you less likely to be like Tesla as there have been countless studies that show declining mental capabilities for someone that is subjected to sleep deprivation. When you sleep, your brain is consolidating memories and building stronger neural connections. You would think your brain is resting just like the rest of your body while you sleep, but in reality the cranial factory is just turning on. A study published in *Neuron* by researchers Dr. Marcos Frank and Dr. Sara Aton of Penn State explains some of the phenomena that is occurring during sleep. When you are awake, your brain is stimulated by the environment such as your professor lectures. "Stimulated" may be a strong word for some lectures, but you get the point. This stimulation produces enzymes that get your brain ready to be restructured, but the enzymes are mainly just waiting around and not doing much work while you are awake. Only when you get some shut-eye, do the enzymes get the green flag to start rewiring your memory. So when you choose to study instead of sleep, you are preventing your brain from storing the information which technically makes the whole studying process a waste of time. There will be many times in college when you will be tempted to pull an all-nighter, especially if you are prone to procrastination (most engineering students are). When this comes, study your butt off, but don't go late into the night. If you absolutely need more time, go to bed early so that you can wake up early. By this method, you are not throwing away all that hard work prior to sleep, and you also have time in the morning to look at the remaining material. Facing these time crunches can take lots of determination, but the learning process is still biological. You need to let the brain rebuild as it was intended.

I have expressed what sleep deprivation can do for your academic performance and what your brain does when it gets proper sleep. What are the direct benefits of proper sleep? In John Medina's *Brain Rules*, he describes an experiment involving kids solving math problems. However, the experiment was not to test their abilities to get problems right. The experiment was to evaluate how sleep could improve their ability to be creative and innovative. In this experiment, a short cut method to work the math problems existed, but the kids were not told about it. Initially, a group of kids were tested with a series of math problems and then retested with similar problems 12 hours later. 20% of the kids in this group discovered the quicker method of solving the math problems after the 12 hour break. Next, a different group of kids were tested and retested just like before. This time 8 hours of sleep was allowed in the 12 hour break. The results: 60% of the kids figured out the shortcut on the retest. That is a 3 to 1 performance improvement as a result of no extra effort except putting on pajamas. This is the power of sleep at its finest. NASA has done similar studies with pilots, which has even shown that short naps (26 minutes in this case) improved performance by more than 34%. So for all you daytime sleepers, science has provided a legitimate excuse to nap. Thank you science.

Internships and Co-op Programs

"The only source of knowledge is experience."

— *Albert Einstein*

Learning with a Salary

I figured the best strategy to get your attention for this chapter is to go ahead and mention that engineering interns and students in co-operative education programs, co-ops for short, have been known to make anywhere between $15/hour to almost $30/hour. That's the equivalent of $31,200 to $62,400 a year or 2600 to 5200 pizzas. That's right. **Students** can make that much money before even graduating. Have I got your attention now?

Several schools keep track of intern/co-op pay. You can look up the statistics on the internet and see for yourself. The pay differs depending on your major and the company you work for just as it does for regular full-time jobs. Companies have also been known to offer additional cash to help with your housing if you have to move for the temporary job. Some even offer bonuses and pay raises to interns/co-ops that return with a certain GPA. Most interns/co-ops are still considered full-time students and can continue to be covered by their parent's insurance. This is possibly the best way an engineering student could pay for their school or even store away some fun money if they already have a scholarship. If waiting tables or delivering pizzas for minimum wage while in school sounds more appealing to you, then so be it.

Others perks

Four years of absorbing engineering concepts and theories can be the mental equivalent of drinking from a fire hydrant during a flood. You are hit with a huge volume of knowledge, but how much of that volume you absorb is not really tested until you use it in the real world. Engineering internships and co-op jobs are not your stereotypical 'mail-room' job. As I mentioned, the company is paying you well and expects real engineering work for the compensation. This is your first chance to really test your engineering skills.

Now don't be scared that they are going to just throw you into the deep end. They don't expect you to be Tony Stark. The companies understand that this is likely your first technical job. The students are often paired with veteran engineers and a mentor so that the newbies have an outlet to ask questions and absorb knowledge from. If you do get an internship or co-op position, I highly recommend you also network as much as possible with other engineers beyond your mentor. Remember my spill about networking from Chapter 3? Networking during your employment allows you to get more insight into all sorts of work and learning experiences. Plus, you never know where some of those engineers may end up when it comes time for you to graduate, and you are looking for a job (i.e. hiring managers).

Speaking of looking for jobs after you graduate, having experience as an intern or co-op can arguably be the best thing to have when applying for your first full-time job after graduation. Some may argue that a 4.0 GPA is better. What if a student had a 3.6 GPA, but already had a one year of experience? Who would be more likely hit the ground running at a new job, the inexperienced 4.0 GPA student or the experienced 3.6 GPA student? That's a pretty tough call. Also, if you graduate and work for the same company that you interned for, they may consider your original hire date and intern experience when determining your starting salary.

One of the best takeaways from an internship or co-op is that you can learn what you enjoy doing as an engineer, and more importantly, you can learn what you do not enjoy doing as an engineer. You will soon find out if you enjoy running analysis all day on a computer, if you like a hands-on environment, or if you like doing a little bit of everything. A comment that is often said regarding the engineering profession is that they "sit behind a computer screen all day." There is no need to argue that statement. Some engineers do sit behind a computer. It does not apply to **all** engineers however. Some engineers are on their feet all day in a machine shop or processing plant. Some engineers are constantly traveling across cities, states, and countries. The idea of an engineer stuck to his computer is a very narrow image of the full picture. We might as well say personal fitness trainers just flex in front of the mirror all day (I'm sure there are plenty that do).

Internship vs Co-op

I have used internships and co-op programs interchangeably so far. The truth is that only a few differences exist. Schools that have an official co-op program generally expect you to complete three full semesters at a company on a rotational basis. Simply, you work for a semester, and then return to school the following semester. You will repeat that until three full work semesters are completed. This will end with the equivalent of one year of experience AND pay. After all the rotations, some schools will grant you a Co-op Certificate that will be added to your degree.

Some of you may be worried about pushing back graduation for three semesters since you will be working instead taking classes. Keep in mind that one of those working semesters is usually during a summer when most undergraduate students don't take classes anyways. You can make up some of that time by taking additional classes during the semesters you are at school, but I advise against it. The extra classes could easily overwhelm you.

There have also been highly motivated students that completed a full co-op program and still graduate from college in 4 years. While this is not recommended, it is possible to accomplish. Having known many co-op students during my time as one and as a full-time engineer, I have never heard one student say "I regret doing a co-op, and I wish I would have graduated sooner." Of course, I don't know all of them, so a few may exist that did regret participating in a co-op programs. Many co-op students gladly welcomed going to work as it provided a break away from juggling five to six classes. Then again, they probably were just excited to make some money again. I was in it for both.

Internships are more flexible as they are generally have no requirement of a student to come back for multiple work semesters. Also, the majority of internships are only available during the summer. So if you absolutely don't want to break away from the traditional fall school semester (it's football season, so that's understandable) and spring school semesters, then a summer internship is probably more your style. Don't think you are not limited to interning only one summer. If you were doing a great job during your first summer internship, then the company may ask you to return the next summer. If they don't, then the experience will make your résumé look great, and you can apply to a different company the next summer. Theoretically, you could intern every summer after your freshman year and get the same amount of experience as a co-op student. Internships are not just for undergraduates either. Graduate students go on internships all the time because a break from academics, receiving decent pay, and gaining experience is great at any point in your academic career.

Nailing the Interview

Since an internship or co-op is likely your first technical job, it is also likely your first major interview. Don't freak out. These interviews are not as stressful as you think. As I mentioned earlier, the company realizes that you don't have much technical experience, if any, and it is rare that your interviewer will pummel you with technical questions. These interviews are more like a first date. The companies want to get know you a little more, see where your interests lie, and generally see if you are a nice, fun person to be around. There are a few recommended practices for interviews that you should use for internship or co-op interviews as well as future full-time job interviews. I will go over a few topics that every interviewing student should do. I will also describe a few opportunities to make yourself stand out from the crowd.

Common (Expected) Practices

Gentlemen, wear a jacket and tie. Ladies, you should wear a pantsuit or skirt suit. Do not wear anything that would distract your interviewer, so avoid flashy jewelry. Any respectable religious or ethnic apparel should be worn at your own discretion, but I would advise against it. That kind of apparel should follow the same rule as jewelry – if it's distracting, don't wear it. I understand that money can be an issue as a student, but interview clothing is important for a student to own. Browse the local used clothing store or ask a friend or family to let you borrow some clothes for the interview. Make sure everything fits well if you can help it. Not wearing the proper formal attire can make you seem like you are not willing to give much effort. The majority of other students interviewing, if not all, will be dressed to impress.

Get your résumé critiqued by your school's career services center. They will have helpful hints about formatting, style, and more. They can also show you how to make your non-technical work experience look good to an engineering recruiter. Afterwards, you should memorize it. Since it should only be one page, memorizing your résumé will not be hard. Also, make multiple copies of your résumé to bring with you to the interview. The interviewer should already have a copy. If the interviewer were to somehow forget or lose your résumé, you can show them how prepared you were by bringing extra, and it would be rather impressive.

I have provided an example of a good résumé format to use below. Feel free to experiment with some of the formatting to fit accordingly. There are a few notes about my example that you should be aware of. Notice how I keep a consistent format of headers (Education, Work Experience, etc.) the help separate themselves from the content. The tabs and bullets are also consistent in style and distance. You are not limited to using a bullet-point style either. Some feel that resumes look better when job descriptions and skills are written in paragraph form. I like to play the engineering card and assume that other engineers like the details to be concise, so I prefer using bullets. Be sure to put your expected graduation date as well. Quantify anything that is applicable such as hours of experience. If you have trouble getting the alignment you need, use a borderless table. In the table below, I have used a table to format my position, employer, and dates of employment. Now if I were to keep the table, but remove the border lines, it would like it does on the example résumé on the next page.

Co-op Design Engineer Eaton Aerospace	Jan 2010 – Aug 2011

Chad Duane Carpenter
1234 Beachside Blvd. Ocean Springs, MS 39564.
228-555-9876 email@state.edu

Education
Bachelor of Science in Mechanical Engineering
Mississippi State University, Starkville, MS.
May 2012, GPA 3.49/4.00

Work Experience
Co-op Design Engineer   Jan 2010 – Aug 2011
Eaton Aerospace
- Designed, developed, and executed tests for aerospace grade hydraulic pump components and valves for multiple aircraft
- Troubleshot damaged motor and pump units and arranged failure scenarios
- Analyzed and calculated various dynamic machine and fluid scenarios
- Conducted multiple geometrical tolerance stacks

Related Skills
- Proficient in ProEngineering and Solidworks 3D Modeling
- Experience with MathCAD, Mathematica, ANSYS
- Knowledge in LabVIEW and C++ programming
- Experience in automotive repair (100+ hours)

Activities/Honors
- Fundamentals of Engineering Exam – Passed
- American Society of Mechanical Engineers
- Society of Aerospace Engineers
- President's List Scholar (3.8+ GPA)

Research the Company

Knowing a little about the company before the interview is a great practice. Take ten to fifteen minutes to look at their website and jot down a few things about their history and what engineers of your trade do there. If you can't find any specifics on what the engineers do there, then you just figured out your first question to ask. Don't think you need to know more about the company than the interviewer, but there is an extremely high chance you could be asked "What do you know about our company?" If you respond with "Not much", then you will likely get your résumé filed in the trash. This is something that takes little effort and time to do. Having nothing to respond with implies that you weren't particularly motivated to work for the company.

Ask Questions

Almost every interview ends with the interviewer asking you "Well, do you have any questions for us?" This a soft-toss opportunity that you should hit out of the park. If they haven't told you already, you should certainly ask what the job that you are applying for entails. You could even ask the interviewer why he or she chose to work there for some personal insight. This part of the interview is a great opportunity to make yourself stand out. Ask about the company's latest projects or how they train their engineers. Ask about how they are being innovative. Ask about their safety practices.

Innovation and safety are typical buzzwords the recruiters like to hear. If you did enough research on the company, you may know the answers already, but this gives you the opportunity to get a little more detail and show that you are sincerely interested in what they do. Taking five to ten minutes well before the interview to go over your prepared questions is highly suggested. Think about the kind of questions you would want to hear if you were the one recruiting students. Then tell them what they want to hear.

Provide Answers

Most of the questions asked by the recruiter are intended to evaluate your personality and how you interact in working groups. The good news for you is that you can prepare for these, and have an answer ready for delivery. I will list some common questions that you could think about. There are more potential questions that could be asked, so don't rely solely on the list I have provided. Remember, what would you want to hear if you were the recruiter?

Q: "Tell me about a time you failed. What did you learn and gain from this experience?"

A:

Q: "Describe a time you were involved in a group project. What was your role, the goal of the project, and the outcome of the project?"

A:

Q: "What is a technical problem you have faced recently? How did you overcome this problem?"

A:

Q: "What made you decide to become an engineer?"

A:

Q: "Why do you want to come work for us?"

A:

Practice Interviews

Yes, you should absolutely practice interviews. Many schools have a career services center that can help you prepare for interviews including giving mock interviews among other services. If you do set up a mock interview, approach it like it's the real thing. Dress for the occasion, bring your résumé, and have your pocket full of questions to ask the interviewer about the fake company. Afterwards, have the career services interviewer provide you with some feedback. This can help you fix any awkward body language such as looking stiff, slouching, or having a scared look like a deer in headlights.

You should sign up for multiple interviews as well. Even if you don't want to work for the other companies, sign up for interviews anyways. You might think this is just subjecting yourself to more torture. My point is exactly the opposite as the discomfort of interviewing goes away drastically the more you do it. Although mock interviews can be helpful, the real thing can still be more nerve racking. After two or three real interviews, you start to become much more relaxed, confident, and get into a rhythm answering those human resource questions. After reaching this comfort zone, you want to do the interview for the job you want. Schedule one or two interviews to get warmed up before the interview you really want to focus on, and then nail that third interview. Think about it as taking a few swings in the batting cage before stepping up to the plate in a real game. I once knew a student that did seven interviews in only two days, and five of those interviews were on the same day. Seems a bit crazy huh? Well he got job offers from five out of those seven companies.

Skills Every Engineer Needs But Are Not Taught

"We spend the first year of a child's life teaching it to walk and talk and the rest of its life to shut up and sit down. There's something wrong there."

— *Neil deGrasse Tyson*

When you graduate, you will be ready to tackle your first engineering job since your head will be filled with loads of engineering practices, theorems, formulas, and constants. We at least hope it's filled with some of that stuff. However, college will not prepare you for everything. There is no "one-stop shop" to completely prepare you for the engineering life. Many skills exist outside the engineering curricula that every engineer would benefit from. In fact, these skills can really make you stand out from the crowd. In this chapter, I will go over a few skills that will not only benefit you in college, but will also benefit your career.

"Soft" Skills

Soft skills, also known as social skills or people skills, can be uncommon amongst engineers. Some people can identify engineers just by their lack of social skills. Some engineers naturally have the gift of people skills. Some pick it up on the way, and then there are some that always seem a little clueless. Regardless of your natural ability, anyone can achieve a certain level of mastery in social ability.

Basic conversation and presentation skills are a great place to start. For engineers, these conversations and presentations can get rather technical. If you are not good at simple conversation, it's hard to expect that your technical conversation will be any better. While in college, you will be asked to make multiple presentations as a way of practicing your social skills. Other than time allotted for the presentation, you are not usually given any advice on how to give a good presentation. The good news is that there are simple adjustments you can make in conversation and presentation to make yourself seem like a natural.

When speaking with someone, obviously you should face them directly. This same rule applies to public speaking in front of an audience. Unless you are motioning to a visual aid such as a slideshow, you should always, ALWAYS, face your audience. Turning away from the audience can make it difficult to hear your voice, give you a habit of reading the slideshow verbatim (your audience can usually read just fine), and make it appear as if don't know your topic too well since you have to constantly refer to your slideshow. This can be avoided by simply memorizing your slideshow, which is easier than you think. If you lose your place, a quick glance to your slideshow is OK.

In conversation, especially when you are meeting someone for the first time, be sure to use the person's name often. This will help you remember their name. You obviously don't have to use the names of your audience in public speaking. However, you should be familiar with your audience in terms of their technical background. Your audience will really stop paying attention if you are speaking in terms that are way over their heads. Remember to bring everything down to layman terms. Actually, you should do this regardless of how technically inclined the audience is. This avoids any confusion on the topic, and makes you a great speaker. The audience is going to be lazy. The less they have to think, the more they will enjoy your presentation.

Your mouth is not the only part of the communication equation. Body language speaks just as loud as your words. There are a few body positions and actions to avoid. To drive home my previous point, make eye contact with whom you are speaking to. Looking at the walls around the audience or looking at your slideshow can make you appear nervous. Keep your hands out of your pockets. Storing them in your change holders can make you seem stiff and unenthusiastic. Some of us will "talk with our hands" and attempt to make certain gestures that coincide with our speech. Others may have different opinions, but I say this can be a good habit as long as it is not distracting to you or your audience. Keeping your hands in a rhythmic motion with your thoughts can keep you focused on your train of thought as well as keep your hands out of your pockets. Most of us tend to have nervous habits when speaking to others or in front of a crowd. We usually don't realize we're doing the habit either. Playing with jewelry, twisting our bodies slightly back and forth, and rubbing our hands or arms are just a few examples of nervous habits. Some of these are not too bad. Again, just don't let them be distracting to your audience.

When speaking in public, it is very important to not talk too fast. It is easy to speak quickly due to nervousness. When you speak too fast, your neck and throat will tense up. You will start to run out of air more quickly as well which can cause your neck to tighten even more. Before you know it, you are completely out of breath, veins are popping out of your neck, and your voice has gone up an octave due to your vocal chords getting squeezed. Not the ideal image of a good speaker. Relax a little, and take your time. If you take your time, you will have plenty of breath, and your speech will sound much more controlled and confident. You will eventually get into a rhythm, and it will be over before you know it. Slow is smooth, and smooth is fast.

Time Management

I cannot stress how much good time management can really help you optimize your day. A full load of engineering courses can really take up a ton of your time. If you want to throw in exercise, sleep, social events, and general life responsibilities on top of lectures, homework, and studying for those courses, then time management is a must have skill.

Time management starts with planning out your entire day. Plan it out on the previous day, and not the morning of. Think about all of your obligations and priorities, the breaks between them, and the method you are going to use to get from one obligation to the next. Are you retracing any steps that are unnecessary? How are you spending your time between those obligations? What is the longest amount of time you spend being unproductive and why? Yes, your time during class may be a good answer to that last question, but that is not what I am looking for. You need to identify when you have the most down time outside of class, and try to fill it with something productive.

For example, let's say you have two free hours between classes on campus around lunch time. You could go back home, go to the gym, have lunch, or maybe study a little. Going back home and then coming back to campus for another class will likely lead to wasted time getting to and from home. Going to the gym between classes is a great option.

Remember, exercise can flip the turbo switch to your brain. Most college kids wear comfortable, gym-type clothes to class anyways, so you could already be dressed to go. I'm still working on dressing like that for the office . . . one day. Maybe the gym is busy, or it's just not a good time. So that leaves studying or having lunch. As studious as you may desire to be, I don't recommend studying much during this break since you just got out of class. You need to give yourself a break, or you will not be motivated to pay attention in the next class. If you were to do any studying, spend five to ten minutes looking over the notes you just took, and then don't let yourself look at anything for at least half an hour. Having lunch is still a good choice, but maybe you want to save a little money and avoid eating on campus. A bagged lunch or leftovers in some plastic wear is always a solid go-to option. Be careful not to eat too much starchy or sugary food that could lead to you having an energy crash. You could be tempted to take a nap during your next class if that is the case, and some professors have found rather amusing ways to wake students during lectures such as squirting them with water guns. Don't be that student.

Doing homework and making yourself study are typically not the top activities students want to do. Homework and studying are lucky to make the to-do list at all in some cases, so don't make yourself spend more time on those things if you really don't need to. Avoid major distractions such as your cell phone, web browsing, and TV. When you need to do work, sit down and really focus on it. Trying to do work when the commercials are on or while your phone is blowing up with social media updates will prolong your work more than you realize. You don't have to give up those distractions completely though. The good news is that those things are great for when you need a break. Trying to work for hours on end is pointless. I found that my productivity and attention exponentially decreased after approximately thirty minutes. I would catch myself just gazing across words on a page of a textbook, but not actually reading and interpreting what the words meant. That is when I knew I needed a break. This window of productivity is likely different for every individual and may even differ day to day. Regardless of when it occurs, this is when you shut the books, turn on the TV, and browse the latest news feed on Facebook. There are mixed results on the research of study break effects. Some research suggests short, frequent breaks are better for memorization but the long mental marathons without breaks are better for problem solving. You are going to be an engineer, so you should experiment with all sorts of strategies to find what works for you.

Complete your daily tasks in the order of how important they are. This seems like a no-brainer, but you will be surprised how often people will take on less important objectives just because they are easier or more convenient. Getting points on the board is important, but scoring a touchdown is better than a field goal the last time I checked. Every weekday for students is typically filled with classes, and you will have to work around those. If you focus on the less important tasks firsts, your motivation is going to get used up by classes and the easier, less important tasks. When it's late in the afternoon and you are ready to relax for a bit, you are probably going to procrastinate on the important stuff. Start your day off with the important objectives, even if they take longer.

Planners are essential to optimizing your day. You can use an old school paper planner or use one of the hundreds of apps on your smartphone. I personally suggest using Google's Calendar that comes with any Gmail account. Paper planners don't send you text messages or emails reminding you of due dates and upcoming exams. Smartphone planners do. Don't stop at recording deadlines and tests in your planner. Set reminders to make your make your lunch for the next day, pay a bill if it's not automatic, or just a simple reminder to take a break from working.

Money Management
Budget – everyone hates the word, but it can do wonders. Abusing student loans and credit cards can really put you in a bad spot. There are plenty of

horror stories of students graduating with 6-digit debt. In 2013, the average student debt was almost $30,000 according to USA Today. The stories you rarely hear about are the students that got out of college without any debt and also didn't receive any help from parents or relatives. These students knew exactly how to manage their money.

I would place a large wager that those debt-free kids had somewhat of a system for their budget, and so should you. Your bank account can be treated just like you are treating the law of conservation of mass – you can't take out more than you put in. Spreadsheets are a great tool to record your different sources of cash flow. Start with your sources of money since there are typically fewer of these than costs. Figure up how much you are going to have on a monthly or bi-weekly basis. Don't forget any leftover scholarship money if there is any. Now add your essential bills such as rent, insurance, and phone. Whatever is left over, needs to cover groceries and gas. Some students may be living a semester at time with scholarship funding or a donation from their parents. For this case, you still need to figure out how much your bills are going to cost you throughout the semester and make sure you have enough. Starting off with $5000 in the bank may feel great at first, but that number can decrease much faster than you think. I have placed a simple example of how to start a budget spreadsheet. There are also plenty of templates, websites, and smartphone apps that can help establish your budget. Remember that a budget is not just a way to keep track of your money. Your bank does this for you. A budget is a decision making tool that helps you avoid financial trouble. In my example, I assumed a student had $1500 left over from scholarship money and parents chipped in another $1000 for the semester. Let's also assume the student worked part-time averaging $400 a month. Be sure to account for items that only occur once and items that occur weekly, monthly, etc. I also assumed arbitrary cost for rent, electricity, cell phone, groceries and cost. This will differ for every student, but you can see how it comes together. Since the only monthly income is $400, then the monthly **net** income (earning from waiting tables minus the bills) is actually negative. If the student drags this out over a few months, the student won't have enough money to cover all the bills on the 5th month. When you make your own spreadsheet, you can play around with grocery or gas allowance to see if you can make it that last month before going home for winter break and asking for more money from the parents.

	Income	
	Semester	Monthly
Scholarship	$ 1,500.00	-
Parents	$ 1,000.00	-
Waiting Tables	-	$ 400.00

Expense	
Rent	$500
Electricity	$70
Cell Phone	$60
Groceries	$200
Gas	$150

Starting Income	$2,500
Monthly Net Income	-$580

End of Month Balance	
Month	Total
1	$1,920
2	$1,340
3	$760
4	$180
5	-$400

I don't wish trouble times on anyone, but there are great tricks to learn when you don't have much money to work with. Being broke can help you separate your needs from your wants. Hopefully, I can provide you with a few methods that will allow you to keep some of your wants. A huge expense for engineers is textbooks. These books can cost anywhere from $50 to $300 for a new one at the official campus bookstore. Then you multiply that by five or six for the full load of classes in a semester. Before you know it, you can spend several thousand dollars just on books. I can't stress how much money buying used books can save you. Used books can sometimes cost as low as half the new book price. I have always gotten good used books off of Amazon. Of course, it can be somewhat of a gamble as you don't know what condition the book is in. Used bookstores in the local area is a good source as well, but the selection can be rather limited. Be sure to shop around online and offline before biting the big bucks from your campus bookstore.

Many states are offering tax-free weekends to help stimulate shopping right before the school year ramps up. Take advantage of this as much as possible and stock up on some school supplies. I've been working through a stack of college-ruled paper for about 3 years now thanks to one of those weekends. Speaking of taxes, if you are working while taking classes, you can get tax credit for tuition and books. This could potentially land you money back on your federal tax return. If you are taking out student loans, start making payments of any amount you can afford as soon as possible. Many times, the interest rate can be lowered just by making payments before you graduate and are required to start making payments.

Being close to campus also has many perks that can help you save money. If you live close enough to campus to walk or bike to class, then you absolutely should. You may argue that you won't use too much gas because the campus is close, but that is still unnecessary money to spend. That also adds more wear to your car, and you don't want to pay for repairs when you don't really have the money to do so. Some schools also have free shuttle services that run all over campus and the local town. You should take advantage of all the "free" things on campus. I use "free" to describe things you already paid for with tuition. For example, you can use the shower at the campus gym to save on water and electricity costs. I practically had a negligible water bill, because I would workout at the gym every morning (remember how that gets your brain ready for class) and shower while I was there. The only time I used water at home was when I was thirsty or needed to cook, which is a whole lot less than the amount used for bathing. Don't forget about the company info sessions that offer free food as well. Studying on campus can also keep you from flipping lights or running the air conditioning at home.

Technical Reading

I've always thought it was weird that public education in the US generally stops teaching reading skills when students go to high school. Most of the required reading in the courses we did have up to that point were classics and typically well written. You are going to be doing a ridiculous amount of reading as engineer. Of course, the subjects will be highly technical and involve lots of diagrams and equations, which is very different from the books you read for those reading classes. Although these texts will be written by respectable experts in their field, the quality of writing and difficulty of the material is usually an inverse relationship – as the subject gets more technically difficult or involved, the quality of writing will seem poorer. This makes sense. Hard subjects are exactly that – hard. Explaining high level, technical topics is really an art, and the strategies behind simplifying them can differ with each topic. You may come up with a few of your own using the study strategies I suggested previously. Regardless, you will face many textbooks, journal articles, and even lecture notes that will not make sense the 1st, 2nd, or even 5th time you read them. There is no foolproof way to comprehend any textbook, but I can suggest a few strategies that have helped me.

With a technical textbook, much of your smooth rhythmic reading is interrupted by equations and diagrams. Sometimes, the book will refer to equations or diagrams that are on the next page or 100 pages before. This is the author's and/or publisher's way of being lazy and saving money on printing costs. When they make those references to something that is not visible without turning a single page, you should add it to the page yourself. Yes, you should scribble in the book you just paid way too much money for. For equations, you can probably fit them in the margin. For diagrams or figures, draw a small simplified version of it wherever blank space is available. If the equation or figure is referred to again 50 pages later and not printed again, repeat the process. It's a golden opportunity to reiterate a concept until you remember and understand it without looking.

I am a huge fan of writing my own notes in textbooks. The sources for the additional notes can come from other things beyond the textbook itself. Plenty of courses will seem as if the professor's lectures are coming straight out of the textbook, but the professors will add their own insight or a different way to view a concept from time to time. When this happens, you should add it in your book. Don't stop at the material included in your professor's lectures. If you're using YouTube videos or Wikipedia pages, insert that information into your book as well. You want to create a single information source that has all the bells and whistles. I would also add the habit of making your single page, 6-year-old equivalent notes (the study method I mentioned previously) as you read your text. If you reread the chapter later on, having this additional information to glance over can really solidify a concept. Please avoid writing solutions to homework problems in your textbooks. If your teacher gives you an opportunity to use your book during a test, a worked solution that is similar to the problems on the test could look really suspicious. Highlighting phrases and sentences is another common practice amongst students, but has been easily misused. Highlighting is not a memory tool, but a 'finder' tool. The bold colors around the text makes it easy for your eyes to find it quickly. Reading the highlighted phrase over and over again will help you memorize it, but it is not usually as effective as writing the sentence or phrase. If your professor does let you use a textbook for a test, highlighting is a good way to find the material you might need.

Try developing a method to keep the position of the line or sentence you are reading such as following along with a note card or pen. As I mentioned earlier, technical passages often refer to equations or figures, although they may not be displayed in vicinity of the reference. If you hold your position while you glance at the equation or figure, it is easy to come back to where you left off and start again. Using a note card or pen can also help you keep a rhythm of reading, which can prevent you from trying to skim too much and not really comprehend what you are reading. My favorite tool was a note card that I would hold just above the sentence I was reading and covering what I previously read. Usually when textbooks do refer to a new equation or figure, it will be displayed down the page of the reference and not before. My note card wouldn't cover up the upcoming equations or figures. This note card was also a way to check my comprehension and attention to the text. If I couldn't remember what the last two or three sentences were, I either didn't understand them or it was time for me to take a break. Usually, it was both.

Creativity and Innovation

Creativity can be quite an abstract topic. It is easy to teach people how things have been done in the past, but how do you teach people to do something that has never been done? Also, how could someone grade or assess students on their creativity? What may be creative to the students may not be creative to the teacher and vice versa. This ambiguity may be the reason most of our educators do not have a clear emphasis on creativity. As engineers, creativity can be our most powerful weapon. Creativity not only helps us take a different perspective on a concept, but also allows us to build our own concepts and predict how systems can work together. Innovation is the result and the implementation of creativity. Remember my example of the Archimedes screw? Going from a water pump to a fastening screw or impeller is a great example of innovation. In fact, some companies are starting to test for creative thinking during interviews. Google has been known for some of their untraditional, problem solving questions such as "You are shrunk to the height of a nickel and thrown into a blender. Your mass is reduced so that your density is the same as usual. The blades start moving in 60 seconds. What do you do?", or "You're the captain of a pirate ship, and your crew gets to vote on how the gold is divided up. If fewer than half of the pirates agree with you, you die. How do you recommend apportioning the gold in such a way that you get a good share of the booty, but still survive?" These questions were for prospective software engineers and engineering managers. This goes to show you that top companies expect a little creativity, so you need to get in the habit of knowing how to use it.

To start your route on being a creative innovator, focus on concepts more than facts. Facts can indirectly limit your imagination and sometimes mislead you to apply a concept incorrectly. As a simple example, think of gravity. For thousands of years, people just knew objects fell to the ground. It was a fact that everybody could test and observe themselves. Nobody questioned it. Objects still fall to the ground, but the "ground" is falling towards (orbiting around) the sun. Because the Earth was so big, nobody thought to imagine that it was also an object moving towards another body. Then people started questioning the movement of the "heavenly bodies." The next thing we knew, the Earth actually rotates around the sun. The rotation was later explained by Newton's gravitational law but was later dismissed by Einstein's theory of relativity. Fact – objects fall to the ground. Concept – objects of mass are attracted toward each other by gravitational fields. Facts and concepts are very different.

Also, you should question any and all assumptions made. Engineering designs and formulas are packed full of assumptions. Plenty of companies operate using past experience and legacy knowledge, and when asked why they do something a particular way, the response is something like "That's how we have always done it." It is really unfortunate when young engineers buy in to this mantra. If you ever get this response, bug everyone until you get a solid, technical answer or you figure out why yourself. Chances are there is a different way and maybe even a better way. This is your time to shine and show the company what a little "outside the box" thinking can do.

Engineering courses are typically loaded with group projects, and many curriculums will round off your senior year with a group-based senior design project of some fashion. Some of the best groups I have ever seen work together are groups that contained various personalities and traits. The diversity of the group allowed everyone to share insight into things they would not normally think about by themselves. Being surrounded by people who think differently can spark creative moments. Think of it like a sports team, and let's use baseball for this scenario. Nine players play on defense and each one plays a different position that requires different ability and talent. Some positions require similar skills such as infielders, but the positions amongst the infield are played differently nonetheless. When you have nine players that are all great at their individual positions, then you have a great team. If an entire starting line-up of pitchers were out on the field, then it I wouldn't be surprised if the event ended up on ESPN's "Not Top 10 Plays". You don't want to be the "Not Top 10" in the classroom, so be sure not to stick yourself in a group of people that are just like you. Don't be afraid to tell other students no if they are asking to work with you but are known slackers. They will ride your coattail as long as you let them, so don't even let the opportunity arise.

Creativity tools can really get the imagination mojo going. These tools simply place you in a situation where you are forced to be creative, challenge assumptions, view things in a different perspective, and draw connections between ideas that you weren't aware of before. As a way to provide examples for the creativity tools, let's start with a design problem: Design a mechanism that can elevate and descend a wheelchair-bound passenger into and out of a vehicle. Now for our first tool: *question storming.* Instead of the typical brainstorming session, question storming is a session where only questions are allowed for a period of time. Generally 10 minutes is long enough. This allows you to cypher and organize detail oriented questions and big concept questions such as "How much does the passenger weigh?", "What side of the car are we loading/unloading the passenger?", and "How <u>can</u> we lift a passenger?" Asking the right question can be very important to solving a problem. Another tool could be what I call a *spider-web diagram.* A large whiteboard or piece of paper is needed for this method. Start by writing your concept or problem in the middle of the board or page. From the central problem, you branch out with the important questions, concerns, or ideas. Then each question, concern, or idea should be further explain by another series of expansions. You will soon start to realize how certain parts of your problem depend on other parts. I have placed an example of the development of a spider-web diagram for the wheelchair mechanism below. You'll notice how it quickly builds and how the interconnections start to reveal themselves. Be careful of diving too deep into detail as the spider web can get rather complicated.

Engineering - U

First Expansion

Second Expansion

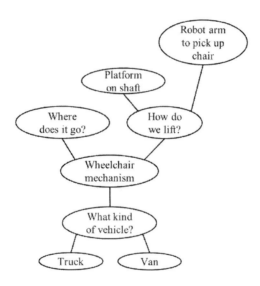

Third Expansion

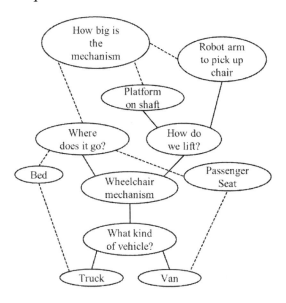

One of my favorite and at the same time most hated creative tools is what I call *finding the holes*. Essentially, this is taking a current solution to a problem and finding all the weak points and potential failure modes. You want to think of every argument you can for why something shouldn't work. I have hated this method because it has ripped to shreds many ideas that I thought were great. In hindsight, it prevented a fair amount of dumb ideas from ever going into play and saved me from embarrassment.

Divide and Conquer

"It had long since come to my attention that people of accomplishment rarely sat back and let things happen to them. They went out and happened to things."

— *Leonardo da Vinci*

The World is Full of Problems

It is easy to get caught in the pitfall that the majority of the world's technical problems have already been solved. Everyone has running water, electricity, cell phones, etc. Unfortunately, this is far from the truth. There is still a large portion of the world that is highly underdeveloped and even struggle for common essentials such as clean water. These underdeveloped societies have never used technologies that has existed for decades. We need to strive to expand the exposure of current technology to countries that need it. If we now consider the remainder of the developed world, our current population is somewhere just over 7.25 billion people at the time of writing and projected to be over 8 billion in another 10 years. Our population is increasing exponentially, and the expected population growth of that magnitude can really strain our resources. Increasing food and energy production to keep up with the population growth are some of the obvious and extremely important issues that will need to be solved by the next generation of engineers. There is also the healthcare we need to provide to the additional population. More people leads to less space and more garbage, so we need to think about civil infrastructure and waste management. Communications and internet demands will drastically increase as well. To say that people get cranky when their calls are dropped or the internet is lagging would be an understatement.

In 2008, The National Academy of Engineering brought together a panel of 18 of the brightest minds in engineering. Together, the panel proposed 14 Grand Challenges that engineers will face in the upcoming century. I have provided the list below. You should really observe this list and the potential for you to make progress in one or multiple challenges. The challenges don't end here though. There is much more to expect in the years to come.

- Make solar energy economical
- Provide energy from fusion
- Develop carbon sequestration methods
- Manage the nitrogen cycle
- Provide access to clean water
- Restore and improve urban infrastructure
- Advance health informatics
- Engineer better medicines
- Reverse-engineer the brain
- Prevent nuclear terror
- Secure cyberspace

- Enhance virtual reality
- Advance personalized learning
- Engineer the tools of scientific discovery

No Job Too Big or Too Small

The challenges previously presented can be almost overwhelming when you get down in the thick of one of them. It is quite unlikely that any single golden idea will fix one of them. The solutions for problems on that scale require a brute force effort from all angles. We can create a larger impact as we add more people behind that brute force. That is where you come in.

These large problems require effort from everyone. Let's use the revolution of the automobile as an example of how it takes a large effort from the entire engineering population to make an idea come together. As the automobile came into mass production, distance was no longer an issue for society. Some people could drive into town and back in a few minutes from their rural home and some would go coast to coast in matter of days. The benefits that society gained from the automobile is practically unquantifiable. However, the automobile is a large complex system that is still being redesigned today. It took years of hard work from countless people to design and build the first engines, chassis, pumps, bearings, wheels, and more to make that system come together to be something functional and affordable.

We can't just stop at the accomplishments that have been made to build the initial automobiles. We also have to look at the domino effect it created. The world had a way to go just about anywhere, but we needed a path. Obviously, large scale highways and organized urban traffic routes needed to be developed (civil engineers). Once we realized we could go anywhere, we wanted to do it faster. Numerous fuels were developed, tweaked, and tested to make an automobile faster or more efficient (chemical engineers). Not everyone could afford automobiles at first. Engines, chassis, and other components were redesigned to make cars more economical (mechanical engineers). Mechanical systems would wear out too soon. We started putting electronics and computer systems in vehicles to make them more reliable, lighter, and smarter (electrical and computer engineers). When we made the automobile affordable and reliable, the industry had to increase the rate of production to keep up with demand. We redesigned assembly lines and automated many processes (industrial engineers). The increase of pollution drove us to find new ways to detect pollution rates (biological and environmental) and produce cleaner cars (all engineers). Paradigm-shift ideas like the automobile provide great advancements as well as additional problems for us to solve.

Learn from the Greybeards

Earlier in this book, I gave advice on avoiding the pitfall of the "that's how we've always done it" methods that the majority of the older experienced engineers practice. That doesn't mean you shouldn't listen to them at all. There is plenty to learn from the older experienced engineers, or as I have come accustomed to calling them, *greybeards*. Most of them are stuck in their old methods, but there is a reason they continue to use them. Their methods, although sometimes lacking proper reasoning, have shown to be successful in some manner. Sometimes we need to try to new things to remember why we liked the old ones.

It is traditional that new hires get paired with a greybeard for mentoring. Take this opportunity to absorb as much knowledge as you can from them. There can be some difficulty working with a greybeard though. When you have worked in the industry for 30 to 40 years, it can be difficult to remember what it's like as a new hire. Keep that in mind if you are having a hard time understanding one of the veterans. Sometimes a new hire can ask questions, get an answer, and still have no clue what is going on. Learning to ask to the right questions from the older engineers can be somewhat tasking, but keep trying. Ask other engineers too, and don't limit yourself to just asking the engineers. The technicians and craft employees can be just as knowledgeable if not more, in certain scenarios.

These guys can be the backbone of most engineering complexes. Most of the work would not get done without their cooperation. Getting on a friendly level with them can make a world of difference for your career. These guys also tend to have some interesting personalities and a much better sense of humor than your normal engineers. They may be able to talk on your level and make you laugh at the same time.

Giving Back to the System

As you go through school, remember all the bumps, bruises, failures, and victories. There will be thousands of students coming right behind you making the same mistakes and new ones. Think about all the ways we can make engineering education better. What are we really good at teaching and what are we lacking? One of the major motivations behind this book is my personal desire to put something back into the system that makes us great engineers. As one person, I am limited to doing only as much work as one engineer can do. Sometimes, I even have to redo that work. However, if I could inspire two or three other students to go into engineering and do great things, then I would feel as if I doubled or tripled my contributions to society. As you go through school and your career, you will have the opportunity to inspire, motivate, and help many students along the way. Pass along some of the information provided in this book. Everyone's path through engineering is different, so you will get to pass along some of the extra lessons you picked up along your own path. As long as we are taking on new challenges and building a better engineer with every generation, our future looks promising.

Made in the USA
Lexington, KY
22 May 2017